Cheryl Harness

Ghosts of the Civil War

Aladdin Paperbacks
NEW YORK LONDON TORONTO SYDNEY

For Kit and Miss P. T.

I gratefully acknowledge the kind assistance of Mr. Bearrs, Mr. Wisler, and estimable librarians.

It is well that war is so terrible—we should grow too fond of it.

—Robert E. Lee, on watching Union soldiers
charge into gunfire at Fredericksburg, Virginia

First Aladdin Paperbacks edition May 2004

Copyright © 2002 by Cheryl Harness

ALADDIN PAPERBACKS
An imprint of Simon & Schuster
Children's Publishing Division
1230 Avenue of the Americas
New York, NY 10020

Also available in a Simon & Schuster Books For Young Readers hardcover edition.
Designed by Jennifer Reyes
The text of this book was set in 12-point Impress.
The illustrations for this book are rendered in watercolor, ink, and colored pencil on Strathmore illustration board.

Manufactured in China
2 4 6 8 10 9 7 5 3 1

The Library of Congress has cataloged the hardcover edition as follows:
Harness, Cheryl. Ghosts of the Civil War / by Cheryl Harness.
p. cm.
Summary: The ghost of Willie, President Abraham Lincoln's older son, transports Lindsey back to his own time, where she sees and hears many things from both sides of the Civil War.
Includes passages from contemporary documents, a glossary, biographical sketches, and a bibliography.
ISBN 0-689-83135-8
1. Lincoln, William Wallace, 1850-1862—Juvenile fiction.
2. United States—History—Civil War, 1861-1865—Juvenile fiction. [1. Lincoln, William Wallace, 1850-1862— Fiction. 2. United States—History—Civil War, 1861-1865—Fiction.
3. Time travel—Fiction. 4. Ghosts—Fiction.] I. Title.
PZ7.H2277 Gh 2001 [Fic]—dc21 99-462276

ISBN 0-689-86992-4 (pbk.)

The Civil War, the War Between the States, the War of the Rebellion, the Battle of the Blue and the Gray, the Brothers' War, the War for Southern Independence: Whatever it is called, this four years of awfulness touched the life of every American. Ten thousand battles, large and small, plus all manner of sickness, cost more than 600,000 soldiers their lives, and the world all they might have accomplished. They fought with almost unimaginable bravery for their way of life, for the Union, against one another and for one another.

In money and property the war cost more than $15 billion. The whole Southern world of ruined land and cities wouldn't recover until way into the 20th century. After 250 years of slavery 4 million black Americans got their freedom—to fight for a fair deal and their civil rights.

Americans of the 19th century were haunted by the memory of their 18th-century ancestors, who fought a revolution and founded a democratic republic "conceived in liberty," yet which allowed human beings to be held in bondage. There had to be bloody justice. This had to be settled, even if it meant tearing the Union of states apart, so we could be one free nation where we, the people, governed ourselves. But with how much say-so from our leaders in Washington and those closer to home? What does it mean to be a citizen of the United States? And how is one's American life affected by the color of one's skin? It's with these questions that the Ghosts of the Civil War haunt us to this very day.

SUTLER
Can't we go home now? This is dumb!
Come on Lindsey! This is like a real battle! Like in the Civil War.
What's civilized about a rotten war?
Not "civil-ized." CIVIL—when people in the same nation go to war against themselves. It's what we did back in the 1800s. North against South.
Why'd we do that?
It was about what kind of country people wanted. And about slaves, mostly.

Hey! Are you okay? Are you lost?
No, miss. I just come to wonder at future folks playing out the War of the Rebellion. Tryin' to understand it, I reckon.
Hey, let go! Where are we? What's happening? Who ARE you? Who's that?
Huh? You mean the Civil War?
For certain. It changed my whole life—my whole family's lives. It changed everything!
How? It happened forever ago, and besides, how could people in the United States be so dumb to war against each other?
Because they weren't united. Not at all. I can show you.

THE STATE CAPITOL, SPRINGFIELD, ILLINOIS June 16, 1858
"A HOUSE DIVIDED AGAINST ITSELF CANNOT STAND. I BELIEVE THIS GOVERNMENT CANNOT ENDURE PERMANENTLY HALF SLAVE AND HALF FREE . . ."
I'm Willie Lincoln and THAT'S my pa. He's making his big speech. We're in my hometown, in my home time.
Oh my goodness—that's Abraham Lincoln! In person! In real life! He's your dad?! Where's his beard? How'd you do this? Can he see us?
No, we're just looking and listening. Shhh!

In the summer and fall of 1858 thousands of Americans came to seven towns in Illinois to hear Democratic Senator Stephen A. Douglas and Republican lawyer Abraham Lincoln of Springfield argue the nation's slavery question in

THE GREAT DEBATES.

ABE THE GIANT-KILLER
OUR "LITTLE GIANT" OF ILLINOIS SENATOR STEPHEN A. DOUGLAS
COLES COUNTY FOR THE TALL SUCKER
Senator Douglas is pretty powerful, so he'll beat Pa, this time, and get reelected.
Well, your dad will get to be president. AND he'll grow a beard—finally!
I agree with Abe. Just don't let slavekeepin' spread into the free land out West. It'll peter out soon enough. It ain't good business.
Pay the owners what they're worth and send 'em back to Africa. That's what I say.
But plenty of them was born in this here country, warn't they? That makes 'em Americans, don't it?

Fighting continues in MISSOURI and "Bleeding KANSAS" where fanatical abolitionist John Brown and his sons hack to pieces five pro-slavery settlers.

There is violence even in the CAPITOL in this spring of 1856 when a Massachusetts senator, who had made a fierce anti-slavery speech, is beaten nearly to death by a southern congressman.

1857: U.S. SUPREME COURT upholds the rights of slaveholders.

October 16, 1859:

Hero in the NORTH, villain in the SOUTH,

JOHN BROWN and his followers, trying to start a slave rebellion, seize the U.S. arsenal and armory at HARPERS FERRY, VIRGINIA. He is captured and hanged.

November 6, 1860: The narrow victory of anti-slavery Republican Abraham Lincoln outrages the SOUTH

SECESSION!

December 20, 1860: SOUTH CAROLINA is the first state to secede. By June of 1861 ten more leave the UN-UNITED STATES.

THE UNION IS BROKEN!

VIRGINIA
NORTH CAROLINA
TENNESSEE
SOUTH CAROLINA
ARKANSAS
GEORGIA
MISSISSIPPI
ALABAMA
TEXAS
LOUISIANA
FLORIDA

THE CONFEDERATE STATES OF AMERICA

What kind of country will we have? The argument is tearing the nation apart.

STATES RIGHTS OUR SACRED CAUSE

JEFFERSON DAVIS OUR PRESIDENT C.S.A.

HURRAH FOR SECESSION!

We got us a president! Hurrah for the Confederate States of America!

Hurrah for Jefferson Davis!

And Abe Lincoln's the president up North—who'da thought it?

Ol' Jeff'll show that Republican Rail Splitter a thing or two!

Liberty and Property! It's what my daddy fought for!

SOUTH CAROLINA December 20, 1860

Hurrah for Abraham Lincoln!
"IN YOUR HANDS, MY DISSATISFIED FELLOW COUNTRYMEN, AND NOT IN MINE, IS THE MOMENTOUS ISSUE OF CIVIL WAR. . . . WE MUST NOT BE ENEMIES. . . . THE MYSTIC CHORDS OF MEMORY, STRETCHING FROM EVERY BATTLE-FIELD AND PATRIOT GRAVE, TO EVERY LIVING HEART AND HEARTHSTONE, ALL OVER THIS BROAD LAND, WILL YET SWELL THE CHORUS OF THE UNION, WHEN AGAIN TOUCHED, AS SURELY THEY WILL BE, BY THE BETTER ANGELS OF OUR NATURE."
He means that Americans, North and South, fought side by side in the Revolutionary War for one independent, undivided nation. And now it's broken.
But why can't everybody just talk without a horrible, stupid war with people getting killed?
Because people don't know how bad the war will be. It's in the future.
Save the Union! It's what my daddy fought for!
I saw George Washington get sworn in seventy-two years ago up in New York. If he knew his nation was breakin' apart . . .
Break his heart, it would.

MARYLAND

April 19, 1861
BALTIMORE
PRO-SOUTH MARYLANDERS attack U.S. soldiers on their way to defend the U.S. capital!

POTOMAC RIVER

July 21, 1861
BULL RUN

WASHINGTON, D.C.

MANASSAS JUNCTION

Soldiers (CONFEDERATE reinforcements) come to the Battle of BULL RUN by train.

FREDERICKSBURG

A FIRST in WAR!

RAPPAHANNOCK RIVER

0   25 miles

U.S.A.
C.S.A.

VIRGINIA

May 21, 1861
★ RICHMOND became the capital of the CONFEDERATE STATES of AMERICA.

JAMES RIVER

At the first BATTLE of BULL RUN, also known as MANASSAS, UNION General IRVIN McDOWELL leads 35,000 "Federals" (or "Yankees") against 33,000 "Rebels" (or "Secesh") led by CONFEDERATE Generals P.G.T. BEAUREGARD and JOSEPH E. JOHNSTON. Nearly 4700 men end up hurt, killed, or missing—less than 1/200TH of those who'll be killed or wounded in the battles to come. A legend is born this day when General THOMAS J. JACKSON and his brigade of Virginians resist attack so firmly JACKSON earns the name "STONEWALL".

McDOWELL

JOHNSTON

JACKSON

No retreat!

Turn back, you coward!

Washington folks brought Sunday picnics to go watch an exciting Union victory, like it was a circus. But it was the Rebels who won the day, after hours of hot fighting, cannons pounding, blood, gun smoke, and screaming. And the war was new, so the volunteer soldiers still wore all kinds of different uniforms, even kilts or Zouave pantaloons. So it was hard to know who was the enemy. All the picnickers and the Federals got in an awful scramble to get back to the capital. They all had a hard lesson.

Oh, I can't look! They're hurt!

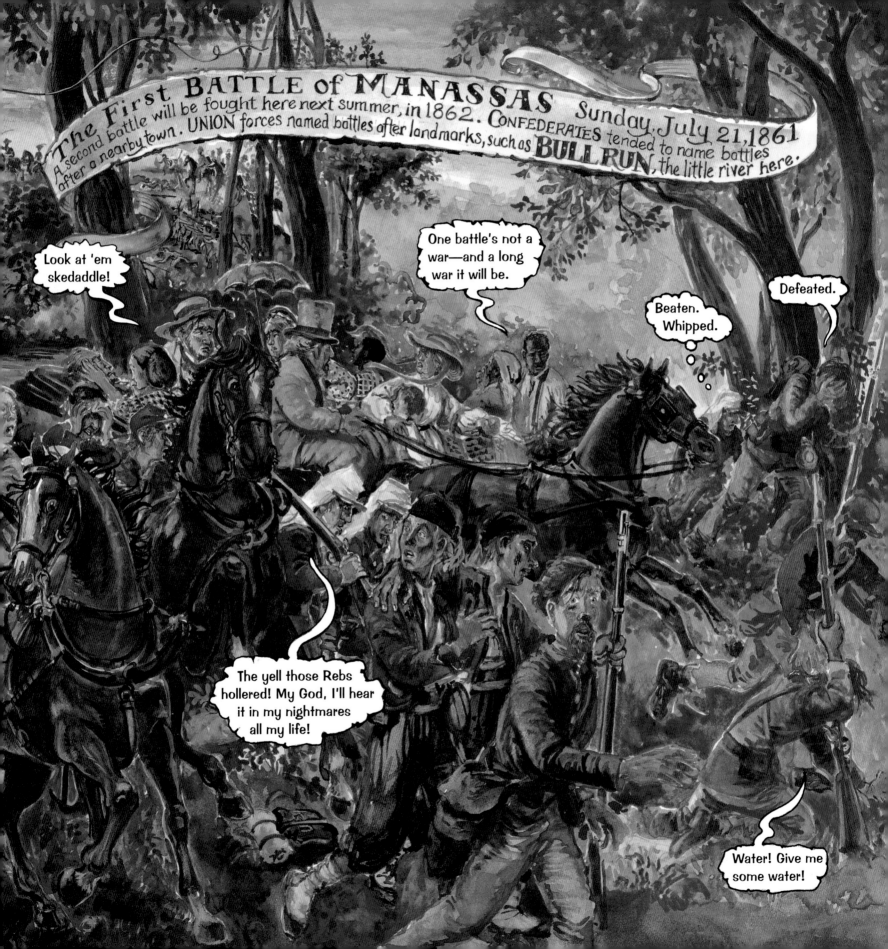

WAR IN THE WEST

KANSAS 34TH STATE in the UNION Jan. 29, 1861

WILSON'S CREEK AUG. 10, 1861

PEA RIDGE, ARK. MAR. 7-8, 1862

The CONFEDERATES defeat UNION forces at WILSON'S CREEK, MISSOURI. However, the Federals' victory in neighboring ARKANSAS in 1862 keeps MISSOURI - with her important rivers - in the UNION.

In all the states along the border between NORTH & SOUTH, GUERRILLA gangs are unofficial warriors. Young men on horseback lead revenge and pay back raids on civilians, their farms, and towns. Especially in MISSOURI:

TERROR!

U.S. Senator JAMES LANE leads murderous PRO-UNION "JAYHAWKERS" while guerrilla chieftains William C. QUANTRILL and "Bloody Bill" ANDERSON lead such PRO-SOUTH "BUSHWHACKERS" as Frank and Jesse James.

EXTRA!

TRANSCONTINENTAL TELEGRAPH is completed Oct. 24, 1861. The PONY EXPRESS comes to an end after 18 months.

Mine eyes have seen the Glory

February 1862. Julia Ward Howe's poem is published. "BATTLE HYMN of the REPUBLIC" becomes the great UNION WAR anthem.

of the coming of the Lord

MISSOURI RIVER

MISSISSIPPI RIVER

CAIRO, ILLINOIS

ARKANSAS

Save the UNION strategy: SEIZE CONTROL of the Mississippi River VALLEY

MEMPHIS

MISSISSIPPI

A grand army is made up of lesser armies. The goal of the Army of the POTOMAC, the great UNION army in the EAST, led by Gen. McClellan, is to capture RICHMOND, VIRGINIA, the Confederate capital. The goal of the armies in the WEST is to win control of traffic on AMERICA'S MAIN STREET, the MISSISSIPPI RIVER.

Who's that? He sure is handsome.

That's General George B. "Little Mac" McClellan. He's mighty smart and proud. Pa chose him to organize and train all the new volunteers into an army to whip the Rebels after they licked us at Bull Run. March and drill, march and drill. I could hear them even when Tad and me were sick in bed.

You were sick?

"TAD"

THOMAS LINCOLN

The U.S.S. MERRIMACK, burned and captured by the Confederates, is rebuilt and covered with thick OAK and plates of IRON.

The Confederate NAVY call their "ironclad" warship the CSS VIRGINIA.

KENTUCKY

FORT HENRY
Feb. 6, 1862

FORT TENNESSEE
DONELSON
Feb. 16, 1862 CUMBERLAND RIVER
NASHVILLE

TENNESSEE RIVER

GRANT

WAR for the MISSISSIPPI VALLEY
When FORTS HENRY and DONELSON fall to
the FEDERALS, the CONFEDERATES lose control
of much of KENTUCKY and TENNESSEE.
The UNION gets its first major
victory of the war AND a hero:
General ULYSSES S. GRANT,
who demands of the Southern
commander nothing less than
"unconditional surrender"—
GRANT's new
nickname!

The White House

I didn't last one year
in that drafty, smelly old
mansion, crowded up with
soldiers and gents looking
to Pa for government
work. It about drove Ma
to distraction with her
nerves. And then—that
winter when I died—
I felt awful, having
to leave them . . .

N
W   E
S

February 20,

1862

Pa and me,
we were each other's
favorites.

My poor boy, he
was too good for
this earth. . . . It
is hard, hard to
have him die.

March 8, 1862. The VIRGINIA destroys two
wooden U.S. warships. SHOTS bounce off her
armor like rubber balls! But the Federal NAVY
heard what the Confederates
were up to and built the
USS MONITOR

OUR WILLIE

THE BATTLE of the IRONCLADS March 9, 1862
HAMPTON ROADS, off the VIRGINIA coast— ENDS in a DRAW after 4½ hrs.
NAVAL WARFARE is changed forever!
As of this day, wooden navies are obsolete.

DAKOTA TERRITORY MINNESOTA WISCONSIN MICHIGAN NEW YORK PENNSYLVANIA NEW JERSEY CONN.

Spring and Summer

1862

NEBRASKA TERRITORY IOWA

KANSAS MISSOURI RIVER ILLINOIS INDIANA OHIO RIVER

MISSOURI OHIO KENTUCKY

GEN. "STONEWALL" JACKSON

SHENANDOAH VALLEY CAMPAIGN

May 4 — June 9, 1862

POTOMAC RIVER
WASHINGTON, D.C.
MARYLAND DEL.

2nd BULL RUN AUG. 29-30
PENINSULAR CAMPAIGN
Mar. 17 – July 3

RICHMOND STUART YORKTOWN

MCCLELLAN

VIRGINIA

SEVEN PINES MAY 31– JUNE 1

N. CAROLINA

BATTLES of the SEVEN DAYS June 25–July 1

LEE

April 6-7, 1862
BATTLE OF
SHILOH at
PITTSBURG LANDING

U.S. GRANT

MEMPHIS

CORINTH May 30

NASHVILLE

GEN. DON CARLOS BUELL'S ARMY of the OHIO

TENNESSEE

JOHNSTON Army of the MISSISSIPPI

GEORGIA

VICKSBURG

MISSISSIPPI

ALABAMA

S. CAROLINA

PORT HUDSON MOBILE

JOHNSTON

NEW ORLEANS April 25, 1862

LOUISIANA

FARRAGUT

FLORIDA

Gen. McCLELLAN's massive UNION army fails to capture RICHMOND because ① he thinks he is hopelessly outnumbered. ② Would-be reinforcements are kept busy fighting JACKSON's men in the SHENANDOAH. ③ "Jeb" STUART's CAVALRY RAID. ④ Gen. LEE's ARMY (+ McClellan's retreat) save the CONFEDERATE capital in the BATTLES of the 7 DAYS.

CONFEDERATE commander Albert Sidney JOHNSTON is killed at the terrible BATTLE at Pittsburg Landing, Tenn. Gen. P.G.T. BEAUREGARD takes charge of the REBELS fighting 65,000 YANKEES led by Generals BUELL and "Unconditional Surrender" GRANT. Nearly 24,000 Americans are hurt or killed in terrible battle: a bloody UNION victory near a little church, called SHILOH

After Gen. Joe JOHNSTON is wounded at SEVEN PINES, a.k.a. FAIR OAKS, President Jefferson DAVIS chooses Gen. Robert E. LEE to command the ARMY of NORTHERN VIRGINIA.

One of LEE's generals, J.E.B. STUART, and 1,200 men, gallop 100 miles around the huge UNION army, capturing soldiers, horses, & supplies— making Gen. McCLELLAN nervous. June 12-16, 1862.

STUART

Flag Officer David Glasgow FARRAGUT commands a UNION fleet of steam sloops, gunboats, and mortar schooners up into the mouth of the MISSISSIPPI RIVER NEW ORLEANS falls to the UNION at the end of April, MEMPHIS falls on the 6th of June, VICKSBURG and PORT HUDSON stand fast for the CONFEDERACY—for now.

⬛ CONFEDERATE States of AMERICA
▬ UNITED STATES of AMERICA

The home of President Jefferson Davis and his family
The WHITE HOUSE of the CONFEDERACY, Richmond, Virginia
Things didn't get no better in the springtime of 1862, not for my folks nor nobody. Out in Tennessee was the worst battle in America ever—so far, anyway. SHILOH. And then General McClellan just couldn't seem to get ahold of Richmond, the Confederates' capital.
Oh, President Davis, so many lost in the West, and now—New Orleans! Captured by Yankee gunboats?
What about this Yankee General Grant we hear tell of? And shan't General McClellan march his blue hordes on Richmond?
And now there's to be a draft? Sir, with respect, is it within the proper rights of the government of the Confederacy to force free white men into the army?
We must wage war, madam. Now, do not lose heart, dear ladies. Our General Jackson is leading the invaders a merry chase in the Shenandoah Valley. We shall outlast them. Our gallant boys shall come home to victory.

PENNSYLVANIA

ANTIETAM CREEK

GETTYSBURG

SHARPSBURG

MARYLAND

PRO-UNION western counties of VIRGINIA vote to break away from the rest of the state.

After his victory at 2nd MANASSAS, Gen. LEE determines to invade the NORTH!

SECOND BATTLE of BULL RUN (MANASSAS)

WASHINGTON D.C.

55,000 Confederates meet 63,000 Federals.

Aug. 29-30, 1862 — more than 22,000 men hurt or killed.

Thousands of WOMEN NORTH and SOUTH work as "angels of mercy" caring for the hundreds of thousands of sick and wounded soldiers. The best known to us, is Clara BARTON, who quit her job at the U.S. Patent Office to become a fearless battlefield nurse.

In RICHMOND, Sally TOMPKINS runs her small hospital so well that President DAVIS gives her the rank of CAPTAIN. President LINCOLN gives Dr. Mary WALKER, U.S. Army surgeon, the MEDAL of HONOR, the only woman to receive this highest military honor.

Legions of ladies like Mary LIVERMORE & Mary Ann "Mother" BICKERDYKE organize food and supplies for the U.S. SANITARY COMMISSION.

Harriet TUBMAN, who had helped nearly 300 people escape from bondage, becomes a nurse and scout for the UNION. She bravely gathers information and liberates slaves from behind CONFEDERATE lines.

Not content to stay behind working in their homes, schools, farms, and factories, some women go to WAR as cooks and laundresses OR fellow warriors, like Kady BROWNELL in the NORTH, Amy CLARKE in the SOUTH. They march along and fight beside their husbands. OTHERS, as many as 400, disguise themselves as men and enlist on their own. Jennie HODGERS fights as UNION private "Albert CASHIER."

CONFEDERATE SPIES Belle BOYD and Rose GREENHOW, UNION SPY Elizabeth Van Lew, and soldier/spy Sarah Emma EDMONDS are among the many who risked everything in the CIVIL WAR.

DOROTHEA DIX — SUPERINTENDENT of female nurses for the UNION

BARTON

TOMPKINS

TUBMAN

WALKER

BICKERDYKE

HODGERS

BOYD

What about gallant girls in the Civil War?

Girls?

Nurse, fetch me that pitcher there, will you, please?

Yes, miss, right away.

HOME, SWEET HOME

Dear homefolks: There was a time when all there was to do was march and dig holes to hide in. Me 'n' the other boys prayed for some real fightin'. We don't do that no more, not since we was at Shiloh. I'd never been so scared. And that General Grant, now he's something. He'd finish up this war if he had to make widows out of every woman in the country! And now that Jeff Davis has put Bobby Lee in charge—now, there's a noble fella—bet Old Abe wishes he had him fightin' for the Yanks!

Slow down! You're talking too fast.

Sorry, ma'am. Well now, tell Sis we hear tell of womenfolk hidin' secrets under their big ol' skirts, goin' off spyin'!

She best not do that! Tell her to keep at her knittin' and gatherin' up supplies like all the ladies is doin': We need socks and something to eat besides hardtack, salt pork, 'n' coffee! . . . I'm surely mighty sorry I can't help her 'n' Ma with the plantin' . . .

I met a tough old colored woman— Miz Tubman. She scouted the backcountry for us. Womenfolk! They're mostly all tougher'n they look, I'd say.

I don't think your sister'd like fightin', nohow. I don't care much for it myself.

I heard there was gals cuttin' off their hair to look like boys, then goin' to the fightin'. Not many—but some!

Mary Todd LINCOLN
First Lady of the NORTH

Varina Howell DAVIS
First Lady of the SOUTH

Up NORTH, the CIVIL WAR is good for business. Manufacturers crank out uniforms, shoes, rifles, and cannons to put down rebellion in the SOUTH AND make money doing it. Food and goods civilians need cost more and more. They are harder to get, especially in the SOUTH where there aren't as many factories; UNION ships keep imports away, and cotton can't be exported. The cost of flour goes as high as $300 per barrel. Newspapers are printed on the back of wallpaper. People follow the progress of the war in publications such as "Frank Leslie's Illustrated Newspaper" and "Harper's Weekly." Folks such as Sarah MORGAN and Mary CHESNUT keep diaries of their own struggles on the homefront. Americans amuse themselves with dances, fairs and baseball, and comfort themselves with songs like "WHEN JOHNNY COMES MARCHING HOME," and "LORENA." They knit socks for soldiers, mourn their dead, and yearn for the day when the cruel war will be over.

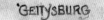

The BATTLE of ANTIETAM

PENNSYLVANIA · GETTYSBURG

HAGERSTOWN · Antietam Creek

Gen. "Stonewall" JACKSON

SHARPSBURG · POTOMAC RIVER

HARPERS FERRY captured by the SOUTH Sept. 15

Gen. Robert E. LEE takes the WAR into the NORTH.

SHENANDOAH RIVER · VIRGINIA

(2nd BULL RUN) MANASSAS JUNCTION Aug. 29-30, a UNION defeat

WASHINGTON, D.C.

McCLELLAN — LEE

N · S · USA CSA

0 5 10 15 20 25 miles

at SHARPSBURG, MARYLAND, begins at dawn, September 17, 1862. By sunset about 23,000 men are wounded, dead, or dying, nearly four times the number of Americans who would be hurt or killed on the NORMANDY beaches on D-DAY 82 years in the future. The day of the Battle at SHARPSBURG remains the bloodiest day in American history.

Gen. George B. McCLELLAN and nearly 80,000 FEDERALS go to meet about 40,000 REBELS in a mighty battle.

Gen. LEE and his tattered troops retreated into VIRGINIA. Victorious Gen. McCLELLAN might have chased them and destroyed them, might have ended the terrible CIVIL WAR — but he does not. LEE's army will march into the NORTH one more time.

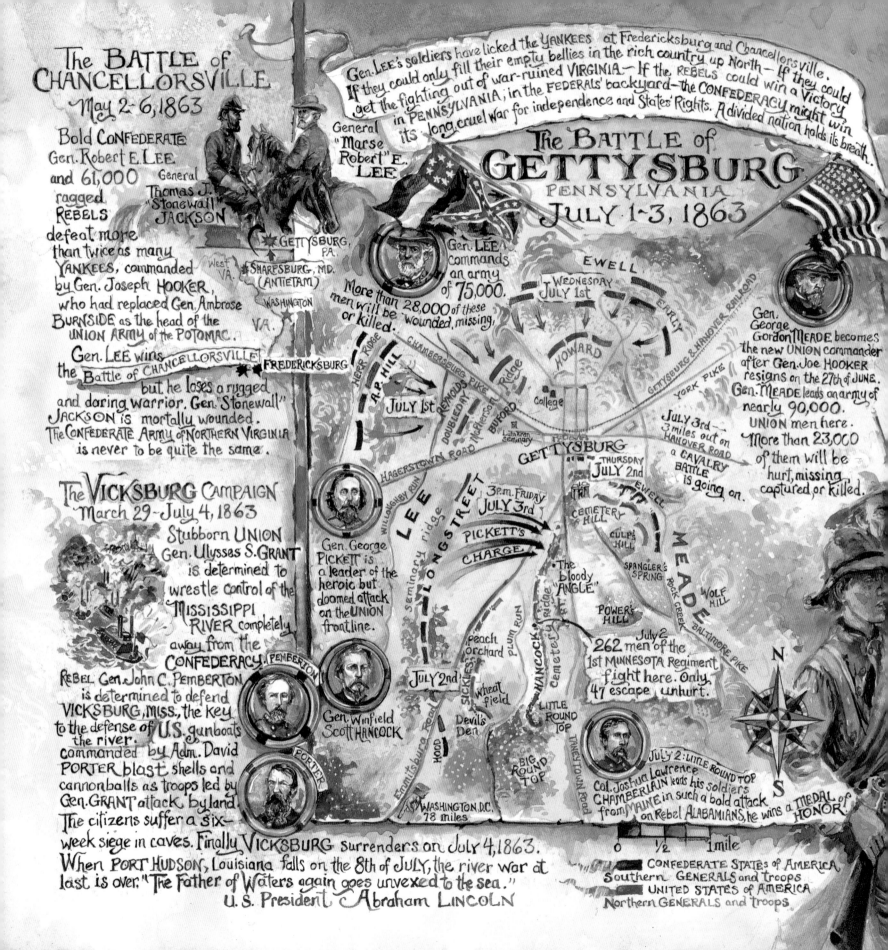

The BATTLE of CHANCELLORSVILLE
May 2-6, 1863

Bold CONFEDERATE Gen. Robert E. Lee and 61,000 ragged REBELS defeat more than twice as many YANKEES, commanded by Gen. Joseph HOOKER, who had replaced Gen. Ambrose BURNSIDE as the head of the UNION ARMY of the POTOMAC.

Gen. LEE wins the Battle of CHANCELLORSVILLE but he loses a rugged and daring warrior. Gen. "Stonewall" JACKSON is mortally wounded. The CONFEDERATE Army of NORTHERN VIRGINIA is never to be quite the same.

General Thomas J. "Stonewall" JACKSON

General "Marse Robert" E. LEE

GETTYSBURG, PA.
West VA.
SHARPSBURG, MD. (ANTIETAM)
WASHINGTON
VA.
FREDERICKSBURG

The VICKSBURG CAMPAIGN
March 29 - July 4, 1863

Stubborn UNION Gen. Ulysses S. GRANT is determined to wrestle control of the MISSISSIPPI RIVER completely away from the CONFEDERACY.

Rebel Gen. John C. PEMBERTON is determined to defend VICKSBURG, MISS., the key to the defense of the river. U.S. gunboats commanded by Adm. David PORTER blast shells and cannonballs as troops led by Gen. GRANT attack by land. The citizens suffer a six-week siege in caves. Finally VICKSBURG surrenders on July 4, 1863.

When PORT HUDSON, Louisiana falls on the 8th of JULY, the river war at last is over. "The Father of Waters again goes unvexed to the sea."
U.S. President Abraham LINCOLN

PEMBERTON
PORTER

Gen. George PICKETT is a leader of the heroic but doomed attack on the UNION frontline.

Gen. Winfield Scott HANCOCK

Gen. Lee's soldiers have licked the YANKEES at Fredericksburg and Chancellorsville. If they could only fill their empty bellies in the rich country up North — If they could get the fighting out of war-ruined VIRGINIA — If the REBELS could win a Victory in PENNSYLVANIA, in the FEDERALS' backyard — the CONFEDERACY might win its long, cruel war for independence and States' Rights. A divided nation holds its breath.

The BATTLE of GETTYSBURG
PENNSYLVANIA
JULY 1-3, 1863

Gen. LEE commands an army of 75,000. More than 28,000 of these men will be wounded, missing, or killed.

Gen. George Gordon MEADE becomes the new UNION commander after Gen. Joe HOOKER resigns on the 27th of JUNE. Gen. MEADE leads an army of nearly 90,000 UNION men here. More than 23,000 of them will be hurt, missing, captured, or killed.

EWELL
WEDNESDAY JULY 1st
EARLY
HOWARD
HERR RIDGE
A.P. HILL
CHAMBERSBURG PIKE
REYNOLDS
DOUBLEDAY
McPHERSON'S Ridge
BUFORD
College
Lutheran Seminary
GETTYSBURG & HANOVER RAILROAD
YORK PIKE
JULY 1st
JULY 3rd — 3 miles out on HANOVER ROAD a CAVALRY BATTLE is going on.
HAGERSTOWN ROAD
WILLOUGHBY RUN
LEE
Seminary ridge
LONGSTREET
3 P.M. FRIDAY JULY 3rd
PICKETT'S CHARGE
EWELL
THURSDAY JULY 2nd
CEMETERY HILL
CULP'S HILL
SPANGLER'S SPRING
MEADE
"The Bloody ANGLE"
Cemetery ridge
Hancock
POWER'S HILL
ROCK CREEK
BALTIMORE PIKE
WOLF HILL
JULY 2nd
peach orchard
PLUM RUN
SICKLES
wheat field
Devil's Den
HOOD
LITTLE ROUND TOP
BIG ROUND TOP
EMMITSBURG ROAD
TANEYTOWN ROAD
262 men of the 1st MINNESOTA Regiment fight here. Only 47 escape unhurt.
WASHINGTON, D.C. 78 miles

JULY 2: LITTLE ROUND TOP
Col. Joshua Lawrence CHAMBERLAIN leads his soldiers from MAINE in such a bold attack on Rebel ALABAMIANS, he wins a MEDAL of HONOR.

N / S

0   ½   1 mile

CONFEDERATE STATES OF AMERICA
Southern GENERALS and troops
UNITED STATES OF AMERICA
Northern GENERALS and troops

The greatest battle ever to be fought in the WESTERN HEMISPHERE, the BATTLE of GETTYSBURG, ends after Gen. Robert E. Lee orders 12,500 men across a field in a legendary attack on the men and cannons of the UNION. Hardly half of the Rebels return from PICKETT'S CHARGE, JULY 3, 1863. The twin disasters at GETTYSBURG and VICKSBURG are the beginning of the end for the CONFEDERACY.

"Right on they move, as with one soul... magnificent, grim, irresistible."
— a UNION eyewitness

Why is THIS battle so important?

The BATTLE OF GETTYSBURG was so huge and fierce, miserable and brave, it was . . . GRAND, somehow. Two mighty armies—more than 150,000 hot, tired men and boys—threw themselves at each other. I think that was so brave! And they were all Americans—fighting against one another with all their might. And all their hearts.

In the long, hot summer of 1863 the U.S. government begins drafting men (who don't have $300 for a SUBSTITUTE) to go to WAR to save the UNION and free the SLAVES. MOBS of poor people (mostly IRISH) begin the DRAFT RIOTS in NEW YORK CITY JULY 11–18.

They attack and kill black folks because they blame them for the war.

JULY 26, 1863

ILL. IND. PENN. W.VA. OHIO KY. OHIO RIVER

MORGAN'S RAID

MORGAN

After 25 days of making trouble behind UNION lines, CONFEDERATE raider Gen. John Hunt MORGAN is captured in OHIO then escapes! Bands of men led by Gen. MORGAN or Gen. John Singleton MOSBY tear up train tracks, steal horses and blow up bridges: EFFECTIVE WARFARE!

MOSBY "THE GREY GHOST"

AUGUST 21, 1863 Provoked, pro-SOUTH William QUANTRILL and his BUSHWHACKERS burn pro-UNION JAYHAWKER town, LAWRENCE, KANSAS. They kill 150 men and boys. UNION Gen. Thomas EWING forces thousands of MISSOURIANS from their homes in 4 counties along the KANSAS border in the infamous ORDER N° 11

TERROR!

MISSOURI homes are burned and looted: BACK and FORTH goes the cycle of violence.

Thousands of black folks were cooks, nurses, scouts, spies, and hard workers—but government officials were afraid of the idea of colored soldiers.

But, Willie, that's so dopey!

True, but 180,000 black fellows did finally end up being soldiers, and 30,000 more were sailors—for freedom, the Union, and $10 a month. White soldiers got $13. Blacks did get more in the danger department, though. If they were captured in battle, they might get taken into slavery. Or shot. Not taken as a prisoner, in a proper way, as warriors.

That's not fair!

No, it wasn't. In the end, 23 Medals of Honor were awarded to black warriors for gallant bravery in battle— look! There, see?

Follow the flag!

Forward, men!

Charge!

RATHER DIE FREEMEN THAN LIVE TO BE SLAVES

CHARLESTON SOUTH CAROLINA FORT SUMTER FORT WAGNER

CARNEY SHAW

JULY 18, 1863 Six hundred African-American UNION soldiers commanded by Colonel Robert Gould Shaw make a historic, heroic attack on the big "REBEL" guns at FORT WAGNER, S.C. Nearly half of the 54TH MASSACHUSETTS REGIMENT does not return and Sergeant WILLIAM CARNEY becomes the first black soldier to earn the MEDAL of HONOR for gallantry in battle.

GETTYSBURG, PENNSYLVANIA
NOVEMBER 19, 1863

"FOUR SCORE AND SEVEN YEARS AGO OUR FATHERS BROUGHT FORTH ON THIS CONTINENT, A NEW NATION, CONCEIVED IN LIBERTY, AND DEDICATED TO THE PROPOSITION THAT ALL MEN ARE CREATED EQUAL.

NOW WE ARE ENGAGED IN A GREAT CIVIL WAR, TESTING WHETHER THAT NATION, OR ANY NATION SO CONCEIVED AND SO DEDICATED, CAN LONG ENDURE. WE ARE MET ON A GREAT BATTLEFIELD OF THAT WAR. WE HAVE COME TO DEDICATE A PORTION OF THAT FIELD, AS A FINAL RESTING PLACE FOR THOSE WHO HERE GAVE THEIR LIVES THAT THAT NATION MIGHT LIVE. IT IS ALTOGETHER FITTING AND PROPER THAT WE SHOULD DO THIS.

BUT, IN A LARGER SENSE, WE CAN NOT DEDICATE—WE CAN NOT CONSECRATE—WE CAN NOT HALLOW—THIS GROUND. THE BRAVE MEN, LIVING AND DEAD, WHO STRUGGLED HERE, HAVE CONSECRATED IT FAR ABOVE OUR POOR POWER TO ADD OR DETRACT. THE WORLD WILL LITTLE NOTE, NOR LONG REMEMBER, WHAT WE SAY HERE, BUT IT CAN NEVER FORGET WHAT THEY DID HERE. IT IS FOR US, THE LIVING, RATHER, TO BE DEDICATED HERE TO THE UNFINISHED WORK WHICH THEY WHO FOUGHT HERE HAVE THUS FAR SO NOBLY ADVANCED. IT IS RATHER FOR US TO BE HERE DEDICATED TO THE GREAT TASK REMAINING BEFORE US; THAT FROM THESE HONORED DEAD WE TAKE INCREASED DEVOTION TO THAT CAUSE FOR WHICH THEY GAVE THE LAST FULL MEASURE OF DEVOTION; THAT WE HERE HIGHLY RESOLVE THAT THESE DEAD SHALL NOT HAVE DIED IN VAIN; THAT THIS NATION, UNDER GOD, SHALL HAVE A NEW BIRTH OF FREEDOM; AND THAT GOVERNMENT OF THE PEOPLE, BY THE PEOPLE, FOR THE PEOPLE, SHALL NOT PERISH FROM THE EARTH."

Because the fighting at Gettysburg was so terrible, people decided to make this battlefield a soldiers' graveyard. Pa got asked to make a speech at the opening ceremony. He did his best to explain what the Civil War was all about.

As the citizens of VICKSBURG and GETTYSBURG are recovering, Gen. William S. ROSECRANS and 58,000 men of the U.S. Army of the CUMBERLAND are at WAR with 66,000 REBELS in Gen. Braxton BRAGG'S C.S. Army of the TENNESSEE. Almost 35,000 soldiers are hurt, killed, or captured in the awful

BATTLE of CHICKAMAUGA
CHEROKEE: "RIVER of DEATH"

a CONFEDERATE victory. "Old Rosy" ROSECRANS retreats NORTH to CHATTANOOGA, TENNESSEE. Soon, Gen. George H. "Pap" THOMAS, the "Rock of CHICKAMAUGA" (because of his sturdy stand there) takes over the troops. They and those of Gen. U.S. GRANT drive Gen. BRAGG'S forces off of the lofty heights around CHATTANOOGA, a big UNION victory.

U.S.A. ◆
C.S.A. ◆

Nov. 23-25, 1863

THE BATTLE of CHATTANOOGA

TENNESSEE RIVER
MISSIONARY RIDGE
TENNESSEE
ALABAMA
GEORGIA
LOOKOUT MT.
CHICKAMAUGA CREEK
LEE & GORDON'S MILLS

THE BATTLE OF CHICKAMAUGA
Sept. 19-20
1863

0 3 5 10 miles

ROSECRANS
BRAGG
THOMAS

The bloody spring of **1864**

President LINCOLN chooses Ulysses S. GRANT to be General in Chief of all Federal forces. Unlike earlier UNION commanders, Gen. GRANT refuses to retreat. Battle after murderous battle, the Yankees push SOUTH trying to smash Gen. LEE's Rebel forces.

Nearly **55,000** FEDERALS are hurt or killed in **30 days** of WAR.

May 5–6 The Battle of the WILDERNESS

SPOTSYLVANIA COURT HOUSE May 8–21

May 11 Yellow Tavern. C.S. Gen. J.E.B. STUART is mortally wounded.

RICHMOND

May 31–June 12 COLD HARBOR In one mighty CHARGE at Cold Harbor, June 3, almost **7,000** UNION men fall.

PETERSBURG If GRANT couldn't destroy LEE's army, he'd set out to wear it out: the deadly siege of PETERSBURG with its railroad supply line to RICHMOND begins on the 20th of June. 1864.

GETTYSBURG PENNSYLVANIA
MARYLAND
WEST VA.
SHARPSBURG
POTOMAC RIVER
WASHINGTON
MANASSAS JUNCTION
RAPIDAN
FREDERICKSBURG
CHANCELLORSVILLE
RAPPAHANNOCK
POTOMAC
LEE
GRANT
JAMES
VIRGINIA
NORTH CAROLINA

N W E S
miles
0 5 10 15 20 25
USA
CSA

"That man [GRANT] will fight us every day and every hour, until the end of the war." Gen. James LONGSTREET

GRANT rode "Cincinnati"

General Grant, the Union commander, knew that if the North were to win, the South had to be BEATEN, or else they'd never give up. He was determined that his bluecoats would fight Robert E. Lee's ragged troops all through Virginia down to defeat, once and for all. He sent word to Pa that whatever happened, there'd be no turning back. Grant and Lee—whew! They're stubborn!

Three years! That's how long it's gone on.

Ol' Marse Robert don't let on, but he must be feelin' mighty low. . . . Stonewall's cold in the ground, now losin' Jeb Stuart and thousands more and he can't replace none of 'em—not like them Yanks. They got millions of fellas they ain't even touched yet.

I don't know, boys. That fire in the wilderness was worse than anything so far. Gut-shot boys burnin' to death in the brush . . .

. . . alongside the ghosts and skulls of the fellows that fell there last spring. I heard Gen'ral Grant cryin' that night. I did myself.

Well, he warn't next mornin'. We just kept on after Bobby Lee. No retreatin'.

We must destroy this army of Grant's before it gets to the James River. If he gets there, it will become a siege, and then it will be a mere question of time.

At least we're headin' south. That's somethin'.

Truly. But so's Grant and his blue-bellied Yanks.

If I was in Richmond, I'd be nervous, I would.

Well, if I were there, I'd ask Jeff Davis to send us some vittles. I'm as hungry as a wolf!

Gen. "Marse Robert" E. LEE sends Gen. Jubal A. EARLY and a small invading army NORTH to Maryland. "Old Jube's" men win a battle at MONOCACY, the only major Southern victory north of the Potomac River. When the Rebels close in on WASHINGTON, "Uncle Abe" LINCOLN goes out to watch the fighting and becomes the only President-in-office to be fired at in combat!

Gen. Lee's horse was named "TRAVELLER"

EARLY

MARYLAND

WEST VIRGINIA FREDERICK MONOCACY July 9 POTOMAC July 11-12 WASHINGTON RIVER

Gen. U.S. "Sam" GRANT sends a force led by Gen. PHILIP H. "Little Phil" SHERIDAN to follow "Old Jube" EARLY "to the death." Little Phil's troops drive the Confederates out of — and scorched the earth of — the SHENANDOAH VALLEY.

WINCHESTER Sept. 19

FISHER'S HILL Sept. 22

CEDAR CREEK Oct. 19

SHENANDOAH RIVER SHENANDOAH VALLEY

VIRGINIA

CULPEPER COURT HOUSE FREDERICKSBURG

April 30, 1864 Joseph, the 5-year-old son of President JEFFERSON DAVIS, is killed in an accidental fall at RICHMOND

SHERIDAN

JAMES

PETERSBURG The Battle of the CRATER July 30 The Federals, commanded by Gen. BURNSIDE, want to blast through the Rebel fortifications: BANG!! They blow a hole 170 feet long, 60 feet wide, 30 feet deep! Poorly led UNION men, black & white, rush into it and are shot like fish in a barrel.

CIVIL WAR-weary and discouraged AMERICANS in 1864 must wonder if the cruel war would ever end.

"Johnny Rebs" and "Billy Yanks" are suffering in the trenches around PETERSBURG.

C.S. Gen. Nathan Bedford FORREST, a tough, merciless warrior, leads his men against twice as many YANKEES at BRICE's CROSS ROADS down in MISSISSIPPI — and licks them.

Equally tough U.S. Gen. William Tecumseh SHERMAN and his army are fighting into GEORGIA.

Gen. Sterling PRICE tries to win REBEL control of MISSOURI.

Aug. 5 Mobile Bay is boldly blockaded by U.S. Adm. David G. FARRAGUT and his fleet. "Damn the torpedoes!" he cries. "Full steam ahead!"

THE CONFEDERATE ARMY of TENNESSEE is led by Gen. Joseph E. JOHNSTON then by fierce, battle-crippled Gen. John Bell HOOD. After Gen. SHERMAN's Bluecoats finally defeat them and raise the U.S. flag over ATLANTA, Gen. HOOD takes the fight NORTH to TENNESSEE. More than 6,000 Rebels die in the terrible Battle of FRANKLIN just two weeks after "Uncle Billy" SHERMAN and 60,000 Yankees set out for SAVANNAH. Perhaps wrecking the countryside would destroy the SOUTH's will to fight — that was Gen. SHERMAN's strategy.

WAR is cruelty. There's no sense trying to reform it. The crueler it is, the sooner it will be over. Gen. SHERMAN

FORREST

SHERMAN

HOOD

Battle of WESTPORT Oct. 23
WASHINGTON
W.VA.
RICHMOND
KENTUCKY
PETERSBURG
VIRGINIA
TENN. NASHVILLE. Dec. 15-16
NORTH CAROLINA
FRANKLIN Nov. 30
CHATTANOOGA SOUTH CAROLINA
ARKANSAS
BRICES CROSS ROADS
TUPELO June 10 July 14-15
KENNESAW MOUNTAIN June 27
ATLANTA Sept. 2
CHARLESTON
SABINE CROSS ROADS
PLEASANT HILL April 8-9 1864
MISS. ALABAMA
MOBILE
GEORGIA FLORIDA
SAVANNAH occupied Dec. 21, 1864
TEXAS
LOUISIANA
INDIAN TERR.
KANS.

Yankees! You've taken everything! Killed our boys and left us to starve!

Your boys did their share at Bull Run and Fredericksburg and a bunch more. All's I know is, between your hogs 'n' kitchen gardens, I ain't ate so good in months.

Gen'ral Sherman's men set fire to Atlanta, then they set out marching across Georgia, trailed along after by maybe 25,000 colored folks escaped from their masters. After about a month, Sherman sent Pa a telegram: "Mr. President, I beg to present to you a Christmas gift—the city of Savannah." It must've cheered Pa up considerable—that plus getting reelected president in November.

Hate us all you please, and think on those poor fellas you Rebs starved to death in that prisoner camp over yonder in Andersonville.

I suppose you're feedin' your prisoners cherry pie up North, you Yankee devils!

War's hell, ma'am.

Not only does Abraham LINCOLN have to save the UNION, on November 8, 1864, he has to get re-elected president of a country that is sick of WAR. U.S. citizens (only the male, white ones) will VOTE for LINCOLN (REPUBLICAN) and fighting on to VICTORY OR they will VOTE for Gen. George B. McCLELLAN (DEMOCRAT) and PEACE—and possibly two nations, U.S.A. and C.S.A. the UNION broken forever.

LINCOLN wins.

The vote shows "that a people's government can sustain a national election in the midst of a great civil war," says the president.

January 31, 1865

SLAVERY IS ABOLISHED! (ended) at last!

The 13TH Amendment is passed by the U.S. CONGRESS. It becomes the law of the land (ratified) in December 1865 when ¾ of all the states agree.

February 3: President LINCOLN and William H. SEWARD, Secretary of STATE, along with CONFEDERATE Vice President Alexander STEPHENS and other Southern leaders meet on a steamboat at Hampton Roads, VIRGINIA.

RIVER QUEEN

They talk but fail to agree on a way to end the war.

March 4: Abraham LINCOLN takes his 2nd OATH OF OFFICE on INAUGURATION DAY. He tells the people, "...With malice toward none; with charity for all...let us strive on to finish the work we are in; to bind up the nation's wounds ...to do all which may achieve and cherish a just, and a lasting peace among ourselves, and with all nations."

Abe and Mary Lincoln

FEBRUARY 1865: Gen. SHERMAN's ARMY burns and smashes north through SOUTH CAROLINA, punishing the 1st state to secede.

Hurrah!

I s'pected 'im to have horns and a tail, way some white folks talked about 'im!

He looks like the tiredest man on earth, poor soul.

Praise be!

In the end, General Lee and his army couldn't stop General Grant and his. In the end, the Stars and Stripes flew over Richmond, instead of the Rebel Stars and Bars. President Davis had fled the city. It was like the end of a nightmare, four years long. Pa decided to go see Richmond with his own eyes.

Look! Isn't that your little brother?

Yes, Pa liked having Tad close by. Pa sat in Jeff Davis's chair and visited with the wounded soldiers.

Yankee soldiers?

Rebs, too.

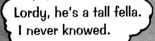

April 2, 1865
After a last desperate battle, the Army of NORTHERN VIRGINIA gives up PETERSBURG. Gen. Robert E. LEE sends word to President DAVIS that RICHMOND can no longer be saved from Gen. GRANT's armies. Jefferson DAVIS and the rest of the CONFEDERATE government flee the city. Mobs of people left behind set RICHMOND on fire.

April 3
UNION soldiers, black and white, put out the fires and put the STARS and STRIPES on top of the REBEL capitol. After four long years, the CIVIL WAR is coming to an end.

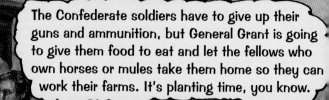

"THIS WILL HAVE THE BEST POSSIBLE EFFECT ON MY MEN."

The Confederate soldiers have to give up their guns and ammunition, but General Grant is going to give them food to eat and let the fellows who own horses or mules take them home so they can work their farms. It's planting time, you know.

Everyone's so sad—and so happy it's all over—

Almost.

What? Ohmigosh—I think I know what happens next. We've got to get to your dad in Washington!

Gen. Robert E. Lee's ARMY of 25,000 men and their bony horses are starving, worn out, and almost surrounded by UNION soldiers. LEE says, "There is nothing left for me to do but go and see Gen. GRANT and I would rather die a thousand deaths." The two generals met in the village of APPOMATTOX COURT HOUSE, in a house belonging to Wilmer McLEAN. He lets them use it for the occasion: the SURRENDER.

Gen. Robert E. LEE surrenders the ARMY of NORTHERN VIRGINIA at 3 P.M. on Sunday, April 9TH, 1865. "The war is over, the rebels are our countrymen again," says Gen. Ulysses S. GRANT.

The last major battle between the lopsided forces of GRANT and LEE happens on the 6TH of April. Nearly 6,000 Rebels are captured at SAYLER'S CREEK.

April 2nd RICHMOND is evacuated. President DAVIS heads for DANVILLE, VA.

April 1st: Yankee troops led by Gen. SHERIDAN defeat weary Confederates.

WASHINGTON D.C.

FREDERICKSBURG

RAPPAHANNOCK

MATTAPONY RIVER

PAMUNKEY RIVER

JAMES RIVER

YORK RIVER

N
S

April 6TH
SAYLER'S CREEK

AMELIA COURT HOUSE

LEE

APPOMATTOX RIVER

PETERSBURG

FIVE FORKS

GRANT

Petersburg & Lynchburg R.R.

Richmond & Danville R.R.

APPOMATTOX COURT HOUSE

Virginia & Tennessee R.R. LYNCHBURG

Norfolk & Petersburg R.R.

Hampton Roads

NORFOLK

0 10 20 40 60
Scale of Miles

DANVILLE

V I R G I N I A

N O R T H   C A R O L I N A

The night of April 14, 1865, President LINCOLN is ASSASSINATED at FORD's THEATRE, Washington, D.C.
April 15: Vice President Andrew JOHNSON becomes 17th president of the United States.
April 26: John Wilkes BOOTH is captured and mortally wounded in Bowling Green, VA.
April 27: At least 1,500 people, mostly freed UNION P.O.W.s are killed in the explosion of the steamboat SULTANA.
May 10: Jefferson DAVIS is captured near IRWINVILLE, GA.
May 12-13: The last battle of the CIVIL WAR is fought: Palmito Ranch, TEXAS.
April 1877 Federal troops pull out of the SOUTH.
The president's been SHOT!
SIC SEMPER TYRANNIS!*
Mr. Lincoln, you're going to get killed! Turn around! Stop it, John Wilkes Booth!
Stop him! He's getting away!
No one can hear you. Come on, Lindsey. It's time.
*Virginia's state motto: "Thus ever to tyrants."

"Now he belongs to the ages."
Edwin M. STANTON, Secretary of WAR
7:22 A.M. Saturday, April 15, 1865
He must have stabbed the other fella.
Willie! My boy . . . Lord, I missed you somethin' fierce.
Oh, Pa! I missed you, too.
Now the cruel war's taken both of us. I do fear for Robert and Taddie and your poor mother. These next years will be so hard—but, Son, tell me now, who have you got there this time?
Pa, Lindsey here's from the 21st century, come to learn about our time.
You don't say! Mighty pleased to know you, little lady. Tell me about—but no, I hear your papa callin' for you. It's time. We've been through a storm, but you tell your folks we saved the Union.
You sure did, sir. Thank you. Thanks, Willie Lincoln. Good-bye!
Look!
They're gonna fire the cannon! Lindsey? Honey! I didn't see you—now here you are again. Come on, let's go get a closer look!
Lindsey!
You know, Dad, the Civil War is a whole lot more than cannons and flags and stuff.
Oh yeah? Tell me about it.
There was this really big argument, see? I mean . . .

NORTH

Abraham Lincoln (1809-1865)

This self-taught lawyer and former Illinois congressman was elected to lead a nation that was tearing itself apart. He used everything he had to save the Union: noble words, a massive army, and wily politics. Days after the Union's victory, "the tiredest man on earth" became the first president to be assassinated.

John Brown (1800-1859)

Outlaw radical "Old Osawatomie Brown," an abolitionist, earned his nickname murdering proslavers in Bleeding Kansas, in a righteous cause. He earned fame and the hangman's noose by raiding the federal arsenal at Harpers Ferry in an attempt to raise a slave rebellion.

Anna E. Dickinson (1842-1932)

Thousands, including President Lincoln, came to hear the teenage Quaker "Joan of Arc of the North" give her powerful speeches against slavery and for women's rights.

Frederick Douglass (1818?-1895)

From the time he "stole himself" from slavery in 1838, this author, journalist, passionate orator, and future U.S. minister to Haiti dedicated his life to the full emancipation of people of color.

William Lloyd Garrison (1805-1879)

Thirty years before the civil war began, this Boston journalist began publishing *The Liberator,* his influential anti-slavery newspaper. He formed the first society for the immediate end of slavery.

Harriet Tubman (1820?-1913)

Before she was a heroic Union scout, the woman known as Moses led 300 slaves on 18 dangerous escapes to freedom. She worked for the rest of her difficult life to secure a better future for black Americans.

Ulysses S. Grant (1822-1885)

He wasn't the very best president (1869-1877), but shy, decent "Sam" Grant of Ohio was good with horses and war. "I can't spare this man," said Mr. Lincoln, "he fights." Later on, when he was broke and dying, Grant wrote his memoirs (published by Mark Twain) to feed his family—a warrior's last act of courage.

Mathew Brady (1823?-1896)

He and his assistants took more than 3,500 pictures of the Civil War. They and artists who drew the war, such as Edwin Forbes, Winslow Homer, and the Waud brothers, did what newsreels and TV would do later on: bring the war home.

George B. McClellan (1826-1885)

The Union soldiers owed much to the training they got from this brilliant military man who had everything but a fighting spirit. He's a puzzle who still inspires admiration and fury! He ended up being a railroad executive and the governor of New Jersey.

William Tecumseh Sherman (1820-1891)

Gloomy "Cump" Sherman of Ohio was one of the few military men who had a pretty good idea just how awful the Civil War was going to be. He helped end it when his Yankee army tore through Georgia and South Carolina like a blue tornado. The man who ended up commanding the entire U.S. Army (after 1869) spoke truly when he said "War is cruelty."

Dr. Mary Edwards Walker (1832-1919)

While Clara Barton was serving as a heroic battlefield nurse, Mary Walker was a pioneer woman doctor. She fought for women's right to vote and dress as they pleased before she was a surgeon with the Union Army, and captured and held as a prisoner of war. After the war she became an author, AND the only woman to receive the medal of honor, the highest military award.

SOUTH

Jefferson Davis (1808-1889)
He graduated from West Point and fought in the Mexican War, as did most of the officers of the Civil War. In 1861 this former Mississippi senator and secretary of war became the first and last president of the Confederacy. After two years of postwar prison he defended his belief in states' rights for the rest of his long life.

Robert Edward Lee (1807-1870)
"Marse Robert" was a distinguished officer in the U.S. Army who didn't believe in slavery or secession—but to fight against his native Virginia was against his code of honor. His mistakes were in daring too much. After the war he was a college president who urged his fellow Southerners to think of themselves as Americans.

Varina Anne "Winnie" Davis (1864-1898)
She was the baby of the Davis family when the Civil War ended. Southern outrage kept this "Daughter of the Confederacy" from marrying the Yankee she loved; early death made her a tragic symbol of the defeated South.

Richard Rowland Kirkland (1843-1863)
He was a South Carolina "Angel of Mercy" who risked enemy fire to bring water to wounded, freezing Union soldiers who were suffering at Fredericksburg. He died later at Chickamauga, just after his 20th birthday.

Mary Boykin Chesnut (1823-1886)
She kept track in a diary of her changing times and the powerful—and powerless—people who passed through her life in South Carolina.

James Ewell Brown Stuart (1833-1864)
Dashing Jeb Stuart was the commander of the cavalry: the "eyes" of General Lee's army. His horsemen could ride like lightning around the enemy troops and find out where they were. He was shot down in a battle with "Little Phil" Sheridan's Union cavalry in 1864.

Nathan Bedford Forrest (1821-1877)
He had 30 horses shot out from under him. He was a fierce genius of cavalry warfare who fought his way from private to general. "War means fightin' and fightin' means killin'," said the so-called Wizard of the Saddle. "If we ain't fightin' to keep slavery, then what the hell are we fightin' for?"

Rose O'Neal Greenhow (1817-1864)
She was not quite as sensational as teenaged Belle Boyd, the "Secesh Cleopatra," but she was a most effective Southern spy in wartime Washington, D.C.

Thomas J. "Stonewall" Jackson (1824-1863)
This iron-willed eccentric general outfoxed the Yankees in the Shenandoah Valley in 1862. He and his hard-marching army of 17,000 Rebels defeated three times as many Federals. More than a century of what-ifs began when he was killed in 1863, just before Gettysburg and the turning point in the Civil War.

Sally Louisa Tompkins (1833-1916)
In her Richmond hospital, in four years of war, 1000 sick and wounded soldiers were cared for. Only 73 of them died: a record! President Davis gave Miss Tompkins the rank of captain in the Confederate cavalry.

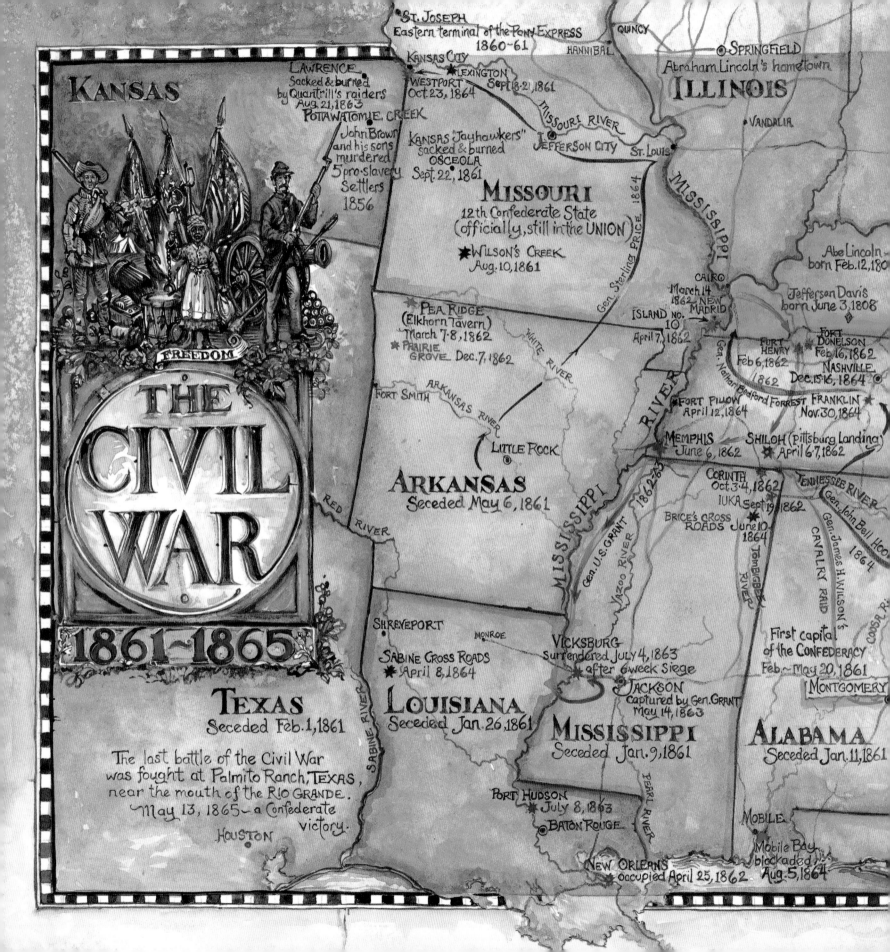

KANSAS

LAWRENCE
Sacked & burned
by Quantrill's raiders
Aug. 21, 1863
POTAWATOMIE CREEK
John Brown
and his sons
murdered
5 pro-slavery
Settlers
1856

ST. JOSEPH
Eastern terminal of the Pony Express
1860~61
QUINCY
KANSAS CITY
HANNIBAL
WESTPORT
Oct 23, 1864
LEXINGTON
Sept 18-21, 1861
MISSOURI RIVER

SPRINGFIELD
Abraham Lincoln's hometown
ILLINOIS

VANDALIA

Kansas "Jayhawkers"
sacked & burned
OSCEOLA
Sept. 22, 1861
JEFFERSON CITY
ST. LOUIS

MISSOURI
12th Confederate State
(officially, still in the UNION)
★ WILSON'S CREEK
Aug. 10, 1861

Abe Lincoln
born Feb. 12, 180[ ]

Jefferson Davis
born June 3, 1808

FREEDOM

THE
CIVIL
WAR

1861~1865

PEA RIDGE
(Elkhorn Tavern)
March 7-8, 1862
PRAIRIE
GROVE Dec. 7, 1862

WHITE RIVER

FORT SMITH
ARKANSAS RIVER

LITTLE ROCK

ARKANSAS
Seceded May 6, 1861

CAIRO
March 14
1862 NEW
MADRID
ISLAND NO.
10
April 7, 1862

Gen. Sterling Price 1864

MISSISSIPPI RIVER

FORT
HENRY
Feb 6, 1862
FORT
DONELSON
Feb. 16, 1862
NASHVILLE
1862 Dec. 15-16, 1864

Gen. Nathan Bedford Forrest
FORT PILLOW
April 12, 1864
FRANKLIN
Nov. 30, 1864 ★

MEMPHIS
June 6, 1862
SHILOH (Pittsburg Landing)
★ April 6-7, 1862

CORINTH
Oct. 3-4, 1862
IUKA Sept 19, 1862

TENNESSEE RIVER

BRICE'S CROSS
ROADS June 10,
1864

Gen. U.S. GRANT

YAZOO RIVER

MISSISSIPPI 1862-63

CAVALRY RAID

Gen. James H. Wilson's

Gen. John Bell Hoo[ ]
1864

COOSA RI[ ]

RED RIVER

SHREVEPORT
MONROE

SABINE RIVER

SABINE CROSS ROADS
★ April 8, 1864

TEXAS
Seceded Feb. 1, 1861

The last battle of the Civil War
was fought at Palmito Ranch, TEXAS,
near the mouth of the RIO GRANDE.
May 13, 1865 – a Confederate
victory.

HOUSTON

LOUISIANA
Seceded Jan. 26, 1861

VICKSBURG
Surrendered July 4, 1863
after 6 week siege
JACKSON
captured by Gen. Grant
May 14, 1863

TOMBIGBEE RIVER

MISSISSIPPI
Seceded Jan. 9, 1861

PORT HUDSON
★ July 8, 1863
BATON ROUGE

PEARL RIVER

NEW ORLEANS
occupied April 25, 1862

First capital
of the CONFEDERACY
Feb.~May 20, 1861
MONTGOMERY

ALABAMA
Seceded Jan. 11, 1861

MOBILE

Mobile Bay
blockaded
Aug. 5, 1864

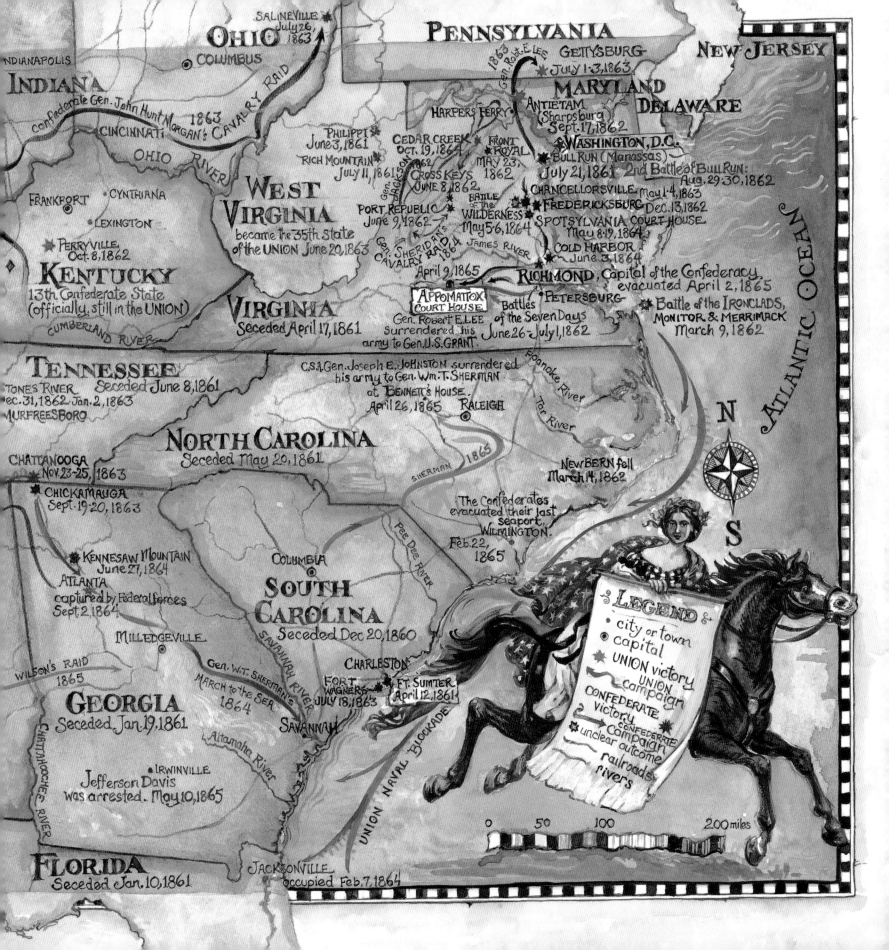

The U.S. flag had **33 stars** in the first 3 months of the Civil War. **34 stars** 1861-1863 after KANSAS was admitted to the UNION, and **35 stars** after 1863 when West Virginia was added. NEVADA (Oct. 1864) made 36.

THE UNITED STATES "Stars and Stripes"

1ST flag of the CONFEDERACY The "Stars and Bars"

2ND flag of the C.S.A. 1863-1865 13 stars (11 states plus secession governments of KENTUCKY and MISSOURI) Some versions of the 1st flag had 13 stars too.

The "STARS & BARS" had 7 stars for the first 7 states to leave the UNION. This flag looked too much like the U.S. flag — confusing in a battle — so a 2nd one was adopted. But it looked too much like a white flag of surrender — confusing in a battle! — So a red bar was added to the Confederate flag in 1865.

The battle flag was designed by Gen. Pierre Gustave T. BEAUREGARD after the FIRST BATTLE of MANASSAS (BULL RUN) in 1861. Because of the lives and times it represents, the battle flag inspires strong feelings to this very day.

CONFEDERATE battle flag

3RD national flag of the C.S.A.

How the soldiers were organized

82 PRIVATES   1 CAPTAIN
1 WAGONER   1 1ST LIEUTENANT
2 MUSICIANS   1 2ND LIEUTENANT
8 CORPORALS   1 1ST SERGEANT
+ 4 SERGEANTS

= **1 COMPANY**

3 to 5 COMPANIES = 1 BATTALION
2 BATTALIONS = 1 REGIMENT commanded by a COLONEL
3 to 5 REGIMENTS = 1 BRIGADE
2 to 5 BRIGADES = 1 DIVISION
2 or 3 DIVISIONS = 1 CORPS (pronounced "core")
1 or more CORPS = an ARMY

Soldiers were organized in other ways too, such as INFANTRY (foot soldiers), CAVALRY (soldiers mounted on horses), and ARTILLERY (men who fired cannons and other guns too big to carry). Sailors fought in the FEDERAL and CONFEDERATE NAVIES.

"I don't believe we can have an army without music."
— Gen. ROBERT E. LEE

Dozens of different bugle calls and drumrolls regulated the soldiers' day. NORTH or SOUTH, they had their spirits lifted by brass bands and drum corps. Musicians also served as medical assistants. But sometimes they made music in battle, "...polkas and waltzes, which sounded very curious, accompanied by the hissing and bursting of the shells," said one observer.

THE arts of death and military tactics were revolutionized in the CIVIL WAR, the FIRST MODERN WAR

FIRST practical machine gun

FIRST use of railroad trains as a major means of moving troops, supplies, and artillery

FIRST extensive use of trenches (soldiers fighting undercover in deep, narrow ditches)

FIRST extensive use of land mines, "subterranean shells"

FIRST torpedoes

FIRST multi-manned combat submarine

FIRST portable telegraph units on the battlefield

FIRST military reconnaissance (information gathering) from a manned balloon

FIRST draft (people ordered into the military) and FIRST income tax

FIRST photographs taken in combat

FIRST military signaling with flags and torches in battle

walnut stock   hammer   rear sight   steel barrel   blade sight
lock plate   trigger   ram rod

U.S. MODEL 1861 .58 caliber SPRINGFIELD RIFLE-MUSKET

GLOSSARY

Abolitionist: Someone who thought slavery should be abolished (done away with).

The Cause: Folks' reasons for fighting. For Northerners it was, generally, the Union, one nation, undivided. Telling the people that they were fighting to free the slaves was not something Lincoln the politician could easily do—not until after the Emancipation Proclamation in January 1863, anyway. Liberty and justice for all has always been the hardest part. In the South "the Glorious Cause" was the idea that under the umbrella of a central government, states (the people) ought to be able govern themselves—and get out from under the umbrella if they chose to. Of course, there were about four million black Southerners for whom self-government was only a dream.

Confederate: Someone fighting for, or a member of, the Confederate States of America (CSA), the government formed by the eleven Southern states that left the Union in 1860 and 1861. Two other border states, Kentucky and Missouri, also had Confederate governments.

Contraband: What former slaves who had come over to the Union army were called. Before the war it was federal law to return runaway slaves to their master.

Dixie: The land south of the Mason-Dixon Line (the border was between Maryland and Pennsylvania, and was used to separate the slave and free states before the war). The song "Dixie" was written in 1859 by Ohio-born Daniel D. Emmett.

Free-Soil: The idea that slavery should not extend into new U.S. territories or states, such as Kansas or Nebraska. The Free-Soil Party started in 1848. It was part of the big North-South split that led to the beginning of the Republican Party in the 1850s.

Rangers: Far from the battlefields bold rangers on horseback raided supply stores, burned barns, wrecked railroads and bridges, and made life rotten for civilians. The best-known Confederate rangers were Colonel John Singleton Mosby, known as "the Gray Ghost," and General John Hunt Morgan. Union General Philip Sheridan turned the Shenandoah Valley into a wasteland. Thanks to such bushwhackers as William Quantrill and "Bloody Bill" Anderson, and jayhawkers like Jim Lane and Doc Jennison, this sort of thing had gone on in Kansas and Missouri since 1855.

Rebel: Someone who breaks away from the established government. Southern fighters were called Rebs, Johnny Rebs, or Seceshers.

Reenactment: When people get together to act out a historic battle or event. It's a way for people to try to experience and understand the past.

Reconstruction: President Lincoln wanted to let the beaten South "up easy." However, after his death the Republican Congress passed strict laws to bring the Southern states back into the Union, get some revenge, and protect the rights of former slaves (for a while, anyway) in spite of the sometimes-violent resistance of white Southerners. Federal troops didn't pull out of the South until 1877.

Secession: Formal withdrawal from an organization. Confederates thought they had the right to withdraw from the Federal Union of States.

Sutler: A storekeeper or merchant who sold food, playing cards, pocket Bibles, and other goods to soldiers.

Uncle Tom's Cabin: An 1852 novel written by Harriet Beecher Stowe (1811-1896). It dramatized the evils of slavery and got people so spun up that when she met President Lincoln, he said, "So you're the little woman who wrote the book that made this great war."

The Underground Railroad: The escape route from the slave states to freedom in the North.

Yankee: A Northerner. Northern soldiers were also called bluecoats, blue-bellies, Billy Yanks, Federals, or Lincolnites.

Zouave: French/Algerian infantrymen. Some volunteer units chose the bright uniforms inspired by the Zouave troops.

AROUND THE WORLD IN THE TIME OF THE CIVIL WAR

BIBLIOGRAPHY

McPherson, James M.
Battle Cry of Freedom: The Civil War Era
New York: Oxford University Press, 1988

Time-Life Books
Brother Against Brother
New York: Prentice Hall Press, 1990

The World Book Encyclopedia
Chicago: World Book, Inc., 1986

Ward, Geoffrey C., et al.
The Civil War
New York: Knopf, 1990

RECOMMENDED READING

Across Five Aprils, by Irene Hunt

The Boys' War, by Jim Murphy

Soldier's Heart, by Gary Paulsen

The Red Cap and *Mr. Lincoln's Drummer,* by G. Clifton Wisler

---

MEDITERRANEAN SEA

CAIRO — SUEZ CANAL

EGYPT

WORK is under way on the 118 mile-long SUEZ CANAL

THE PONY EXPRESS 10 day MAIL! ST. JOSEPH, MO. to SACRAMENTO, CA. April 3, 1860 ~ October 26, 1861

TRANSCONTINENTAL TELEGRAPH!! OCT. 24, 1861

TRANSATLANTIC TELEGRAPH CABLE on the ocean floor by 1866!

1860 ÉTIENNE LENOIR builds the first practical INTERNAL-COMBUSTION engine.

People are hard at work on the TRANSCONTINENTAL RAILROAD.

Feb. 10, 1863

Miss WARREN and "Gen. Tom THUMB," a little person in P.T. BARNUM'S CIRCUS, have a BIG wedding

BASEBALL-playing UNION soldiers spread the new sport around the country.

1861 "GREAT EXPECTATIONS" Charles Dickens

1863 : "HOSPITAL SKETCHES" Louisa May Alcott writes about her time as a nurse in the UNION ARMY

1865 : ALICE's ADVENTURES IN WONDERLAND LEWIS CARROLL

FRANCE invades MEXICO! 1862-1863

·1862· The SIOUX UPRISING Starving LAKOTA people raid and kill white settlers in MINNESOTA. President LINCOLN orders the hangings of 38 INDIAN leaders.

Queen *Victoria* reigns over the Empire of GREAT BRITAIN 1837-1901

1860-1861 Giuseppe GARIBALDI leads 1,000 "RED SHIRTS" in battle to unite his country: THE KINGDOM of ITALY is formed.

1861 CZAR ALEXANDER II frees the SERFS, RUSSIAN peasants bound to work land owned by the aristocrats.

EMPRESS TZU-HSI reigns (1862-1908) over a troubled CHINA millions die in bloody uprisings. 1851-1864